THE BURGER JOURNAL

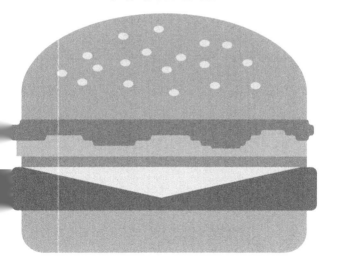

THE GOLDEN AGE OF NOTEBOOKS™

ABOUT

THIS BURGER JOURNAL IS OWNED BY

**IF THIS JOURNAL IS LOST, PLEASE BE
SO KIND AS TO RETURN IT TO / CONTACT**

REWARD
○ YES
○ NO
○ MAYBE

START DATE

END DATE

THE GOLDEN AGE OF NOTEBOOKS IS AN IMPRINT OF THE PRODUCTIVE LUDDITE.
COPYRIGHT © 2013 THE PRODUCTIVE LUDDITE. VISIT: PRODUCTIVELUDDITE.COM

HOW TO USE
THE BURGER JOURNAL

You are passionate about burgers. THE GOLDEN AGE OF NOTEBOOKS gets that. *The Burger Journal* helps you keep a record of your hamburger adventures.

NAME OF HAMBURGER	What do they call the hamburger?
MAKER	Who made the burger? The answer may be the name of a restaurant or the name of someone you know.
TOPPINGS	What toppings were on the burger? Were the toppings classics like lettuce, onions, bacon, pickles, tomato, or cheese? Or something more exotic
CONDIMENTS	What condiments were on the burger? Ketchup, mustard, mayo, or BBQ sauce, or something else?
TYPE OF BEEF	Was the burger made up of ground beef? Kobe beef? Angus beef? Something else?
SEASONING	Was the beef made tasty by virtue of a seasoning on the beef?
TYPE OF BUN	What kind of bun was the burger served on?
WEIGHT/CALORIES	How much did the burger weight in at? How many calories was it?
COOKED	Was the burger cooked rare, medium, or well-done? Was it overdone or underdone?
COST	How much did the burger cost?
SIDES	What sides came with the burger? Fries? Salad? Other?
REVIEW	What did you think of the burger? Use this section to write down exactly what you think.
NOTES	Did you take special note of something about this burger, the restaurant, the service, who you ate with? Whatever the question, the notes section has room for the answer.

BEST BURGER JOINTS

THE JOINT	THE BURGER

NAME OF HAMBURGER

MAKER

TOPPINGS
- ◯ LETTUCE ◯ ONION
- ◯ BACON ◯ PICKLES
- ◯ TOMATO ◯ CHEESE

TYPE OF BEEF

TYPE OF BUN

SEASONING

WEIGHT/CALORIES

COOKED

SIDES

COST

CONDIMENTS
- ◯ KETCHUP
- ◯ MUSTARD
- ◯ MAYONAISE
- ◯ BBQ SAUCE

REVIEW

☆☆☆☆☆

NOTES

Hamburger Review

NAME OF HAMBURGER

MAKER

TOPPINGS
- ◯ LETTUCE
- ◯ ONION
- ◯ BACON
- ◯ PICKLES
- ◯ TOMATO
- ◯ CHEESE

TYPE OF BEEF

TYPE OF BUN

SEASONING

WEIGHT/CALORIES

COOKED

SIDES

COST

CONDIMENTS
- ◯ KETCHUP
- ◯ MUSTARD
- ◯ MAYONAISE
- ◯ BBQ SAUCE

REVIEW　　　☆☆☆☆☆

NOTES

NAME OF HAMBURGER

MAKER

TOPPINGS
- ◯ LETTUCE ◯ ONION
- ◯ BACON ◯ PICKLES
- ◯ TOMATO ◯ CHEESE

TYPE OF BEEF

TYPE OF BUN

SEASONING

WEIGHT/CALORIES

COOKED

SIDES

COST

CONDIMENTS
- ◯ KETCHUP
- ◯ MUSTARD
- ◯ MAYONAISE
- ◯ BBQ SAUCE

REVIEW

☆☆☆☆☆

NOTES

Hamburger Review

NAME OF HAMBURGER

MAKER

TOPPINGS
- ◯ LETTUCE
- ◯ ONION
- ◯ BACON
- ◯ PICKLES
- ◯ TOMATO
- ◯ CHEESE

TYPE OF BEEF

TYPE OF BUN

SEASONING

WEIGHT/CALORIES

COOKED

SIDES

COST

CONDIMENTS
- ◯ KETCHUP
- ◯ MUSTARD
- ◯ MAYONAISE
- ◯ BBQ SAUCE

REVIEW   ☆☆☆☆☆

NOTES

NAME OF HAMBURGER

MAKER

TOPPINGS
- ( ) LETTUCE ( ) ONION
- ( ) BACON ( ) PICKLES
- ( ) TOMATO ( ) CHEESE

TYPE OF BEEF

TYPE OF BUN

SEASONING

WEIGHT/CALORIES

COOKED

SIDES

COST

CONDIMENTS
- ( ) KETCHUP
- ( ) MUSTARD
- ( ) MAYONAISE
- ( ) BBQ SAUCE

REVIEW

☆☆☆☆☆

NOTES

NAME OF HAMBURGER

MAKER

TOPPINGS
- ( ) LETTUCE ( ) ONION
- ( ) BACON ( ) PICKLES
- ( ) TOMATO ( ) CHEESE

TYPE OF BEEF

TYPE OF BUN

SEASONING

WEIGHT/CALORIES

COOKED

SIDES

COST

CONDIMENTS
- ( ) KETCHUP
- ( ) MUSTARD
- ( ) MAYONAISE
- ( ) BBQ SAUCE

REVIEW

☆☆☆☆☆

NOTES

NAME OF HAMBURGER

MAKER

TOPPINGS
- ◯ LETTUCE
- ◯ ONION
- ◯ BACON
- ◯ PICKLES
- ◯ TOMATO
- ◯ CHEESE

TYPE OF BEEF

SEASONING

COOKED

COST

TYPE OF BUN

WEIGHT/CALORIES

SIDES

CONDIMENTS
- ◯ KETCHUP
- ◯ MUSTARD
- ◯ MAYONAISE
- ◯ BBQ SAUCE

REVIEW

☆☆☆☆☆

NOTES

NAME OF HAMBURGER

MAKER

TOPPINGS
- ◯ LETTUCE ◯ ONION
- ◯ BACON   ◯ PICKLES
- ◯ TOMATO   ◯ CHEESE

TYPE OF BEEF

TYPE OF BUN

SEASONING

WEIGHT/CALORIES

COOKED

SIDES

COST

CONDIMENTS
- ◯ KETCHUP
- ◯ MUSTARD
- ◯ MAYONAISE
- ◯ BBQ SAUCE

REVIEW

☆☆☆☆☆

NOTES

NAME OF HAMBURGER

MAKER

TOPPINGS
- ⚪ LETTUCE
- ⚪ ONION
- ⚪ BACON
- ⚪ PICKLES
- ⚪ TOMATO
- ⚪ CHEESE

TYPE OF BEEF

TYPE OF BUN

SEASONING

WEIGHT/CALORIES

COOKED

SIDES

COST

CONDIMENTS
- ⚪ KETCHUP
- ⚪ MUSTARD
- ⚪ MAYONAISE
- ⚪ BBQ SAUCE

REVIEW

☆☆☆☆☆

NOTES

Hamburger Log

NAME OF HAMBURGER

MAKER

TOPPINGS
- ◯ LETTUCE
- ◯ ONION
- ◯ BACON
- ◯ PICKLES
- ◯ TOMATO
- ◯ CHEESE

TYPE OF BEEF

TYPE OF BUN

SEASONING

WEIGHT/CALORIES

COOKED

SIDES

COST

CONDIMENTS
- ◯ KETCHUP
- ◯ MUSTARD
- ◯ MAYONAISE
- ◯ BBQ SAUCE

REVIEW

☆☆☆☆☆

NOTES

NAME OF HAMBURGER

MAKER

TOPPINGS
- ( ) LETTUCE ( ) ONION
- ( ) BACON ( ) PICKLES
- ( ) TOMATO ( ) CHEESE

TYPE OF BEEF

TYPE OF BUN

SEASONING

WEIGHT/CALORIES

COOKED

SIDES

COST

CONDIMENTS
- ( ) KETCHUP
- ( ) MUSTARD
- ( ) MAYONAISE
- ( ) BBQ SAUCE

REVIEW

☆☆☆☆☆

NOTES

NAME OF HAMBURGER		MAKER

TOPPINGS
- ○ LETTUCE
- ○ ONION
- ○ BACON
- ○ PICKLES
- ○ TOMATO
- ○ CHEESE

TYPE OF BEEF

TYPE OF BUN

SEASONING

WEIGHT/CALORIES

COOKED

SIDES

COST

CONDIMENTS
- ○ KETCHUP
- ○ MUSTARD
- ○ MAYONAISE
- ○ BBQ SAUCE

REVIEW   ☆☆☆☆☆

NOTES

NAME OF HAMBURGER

MAKER

TOPPINGS
- ( ) LETTUCE ( ) ONION
- ( ) BACON ( ) PICKLES
- ( ) TOMATO ( ) CHEESE

TYPE OF BEEF

TYPE OF BUN

SEASONING

WEIGHT/CALORIES

COOKED

SIDES

COST

CONDIMENTS
- ( ) KETCHUP
- ( ) MUSTARD
- ( ) MAYONAISE
- ( ) BBQ SAUCE

REVIEW

☆☆☆☆☆

NOTES

NAME OF HAMBURGER

MAKER

TOPPINGS
- ( ) LETTUCE ( ) ONION
- ( ) BACON ( ) PICKLES
- ( ) TOMATO ( ) CHEESE

TYPE OF BEEF

TYPE OF BUN

SEASONING

WEIGHT/CALORIES

COOKED

SIDES

COST

CONDIMENTS
- ( ) KETCHUP
- ( ) MUSTARD
- ( ) MAYONAISE
- ( ) BBQ SAUCE

REVIEW

☆☆☆☆☆

NOTES

NAME OF HAMBURGER

MAKER

TOPPINGS
- ( ) LETTUCE ( ) ONION
- ( ) BACON ( ) PICKLES
- ( ) TOMATO ( ) CHEESE

TYPE OF BEEF

TYPE OF BUN

SEASONING

WEIGHT/CALORIES

COOKED

SIDES

COST

CONDIMENTS
- ( ) KETCHUP
- ( ) MUSTARD
- ( ) MAYONAISE
- ( ) BBQ SAUCE

REVIEW

☆☆☆☆☆

NOTES

NAME OF HAMBURGER

MAKER

TOPPINGS
- ( ) LETTUCE ( ) ONION
- ( ) BACON ( ) PICKLES
- ( ) TOMATO ( ) CHEESE

TYPE OF BEEF

TYPE OF BUN

SEASONING

WEIGHT/CALORIES

COOKED

SIDES

COST

CONDIMENTS
- ( ) KETCHUP
- ( ) MUSTARD
- ( ) MAYONAISE
- ( ) BBQ SAUCE

REVIEW

☆☆☆☆☆

NOTES

NAME OF HAMBURGER

MAKER

TOPPINGS
- ⭘ LETTUCE ⭘ ONION
- ⭘ BACON   ⭘ PICKLES
- ⭘ TOMATO   ⭘ CHEESE

TYPE OF BEEF

TYPE OF BUN

SEASONING

WEIGHT/CALORIES

COOKED

SIDES

COST

CONDIMENTS
- ⭘ KETCHUP
- ⭘ MUSTARD
- ⭘ MAYONAISE
- ⭘ BBQ SAUCE

REVIEW   ☆ ☆ ☆ ☆ ☆

NOTES

NAME OF HAMBURGER

MAKER

TOPPINGS
- ○ LETTUCE
- ○ ONION
- ○ BACON
- ○ PICKLES
- ○ TOMATO
- ○ CHEESE

TYPE OF BEEF

TYPE OF BUN

SEASONING

WEIGHT/CALORIES

COOKED

SIDES

COST

CONDIMENTS
- ○ KETCHUP
- ○ MUSTARD
- ○ MAYONAISE
- ○ BBQ SAUCE

REVIEW

☆☆☆☆☆

NOTES

NAME OF HAMBURGER

MAKER

TOPPINGS
- ◯ LETTUCE ◯ ONION
- ◯ BACON ◯ PICKLES
- ◯ TOMATO ◯ CHEESE

TYPE OF BEEF

TYPE OF BUN

SEASONING

WEIGHT/CALORIES

COOKED

SIDES

COST

CONDIMENTS
- ◯ KETCHUP
- ◯ MUSTARD
- ◯ MAYONAISE
- ◯ BBQ SAUCE

REVIEW ☆☆☆☆☆

NOTES

NAME OF HAMBURGER

MAKER

TOPPINGS
- ◯ LETTUCE ◯ ONION
- ◯ BACON ◯ PICKLES
- ◯ TOMATO ◯ CHEESE

TYPE OF BEEF

TYPE OF BUN

SEASONING

WEIGHT/CALORIES

COOKED

SIDES

COST

CONDIMENTS
- ◯ KETCHUP
- ◯ MUSTARD
- ◯ MAYONAISE
- ◯ BBQ SAUCE

REVIEW

☆ ☆ ☆ ☆ ☆

NOTES

NAME OF HAMBURGER

MAKER

TOPPINGS
- ( ) LETTUCE ( ) ONION
- ( ) BACON ( ) PICKLES
- ( ) TOMATO ( ) CHEESE

TYPE OF BEEF

TYPE OF BUN

SEASONING

WEIGHT/CALORIES

COOKED

SIDES

COST

CONDIMENTS
- ( ) KETCHUP
- ( ) MUSTARD
- ( ) MAYONAISE
- ( ) BBQ SAUCE

REVIEW

☆☆☆☆☆

NOTES

NAME OF HAMBURGER

MAKER

TOPPINGS
- ○ LETTUCE
- ○ ONION
- ○ BACON
- ○ PICKLES
- ○ TOMATO
- ○ CHEESE

TYPE OF BEEF

TYPE OF BUN

SEASONING

WEIGHT/CALORIES

COOKED

SIDES

COST

CONDIMENTS
- ○ KETCHUP
- ○ MUSTARD
- ○ MAYONAISE
- ○ BBQ SAUCE

REVIEW

☆☆☆☆☆

NOTES

NAME OF HAMBURGER

MAKER

TOPPINGS
- ◯ LETTUCE ◯ ONION
- ◯ BACON ◯ PICKLES
- ◯ TOMATO ◯ CHEESE

TYPE OF BEEF

TYPE OF BUN

SEASONING

WEIGHT/CALORIES

COOKED

SIDES

COST

CONDIMENTS
- ◯ KETCHUP
- ◯ MUSTARD
- ◯ MAYONAISE
- ◯ BBQ SAUCE

REVIEW ☆☆☆☆☆

NOTES

NAME OF HAMBURGER

MAKER

TOPPINGS
- ( ) LETTUCE
- ( ) ONION
- ( ) BACON
- ( ) PICKLES
- ( ) TOMATO
- ( ) CHEESE

TYPE OF BEEF

TYPE OF BUN

SEASONING

WEIGHT/CALORIES

COOKED

SIDES

COST

CONDIMENTS
- ( ) KETCHUP
- ( ) MUSTARD
- ( ) MAYONAISE
- ( ) BBQ SAUCE

REVIEW

☆ ☆ ☆ ☆ ☆

NOTES

NAME OF HAMBURGER

MAKER

TOPPINGS
- ○ LETTUCE
- ○ ONION
- ○ BACON
- ○ PICKLES
- ○ TOMATO
- ○ CHEESE

TYPE OF BEEF

TYPE OF BUN

SEASONING

WEIGHT/CALORIES

COOKED

SIDES

COST

CONDIMENTS
- ○ KETCHUP
- ○ MUSTARD
- ○ MAYONAISE
- ○ BBQ SAUCE

REVIEW

☆☆☆☆☆

NOTES

NAME OF HAMBURGER

MAKER

TOPPINGS
- ( ) LETTUCE
- ( ) ONION
- ( ) BACON
- ( ) PICKLES
- ( ) TOMATO
- ( ) CHEESE

TYPE OF BEEF

TYPE OF BUN

SEASONING

WEIGHT/CALORIES

COOKED

SIDES

COST

CONDIMENTS
- ( ) KETCHUP
- ( ) MUSTARD
- ( ) MAYONAISE
- ( ) BBQ SAUCE

REVIEW ☆☆☆☆☆

NOTES

NAME OF HAMBURGER

MAKER

TOPPINGS
- ◯ LETTUCE
- ◯ ONION
- ◯ BACON
- ◯ PICKLES
- ◯ TOMATO
- ◯ CHEESE

TYPE OF BEEF

TYPE OF BUN

SEASONING

WEIGHT/CALORIES

COOKED

SIDES

COST

CONDIMENTS
- ◯ KETCHUP
- ◯ MUSTARD
- ◯ MAYONAISE
- ◯ BBQ SAUCE

REVIEW   ☆☆☆☆☆

NOTES

NAME OF HAMBURGER

MAKER

TOPPINGS
- ◯ LETTUCE ◯ ONION
- ◯ BACON ◯ PICKLES
- ◯ TOMATO ◯ CHEESE

TYPE OF BEEF

TYPE OF BUN

SEASONING

WEIGHT/CALORIES

COOKED

SIDES

COST

CONDIMENTS
- ◯ KETCHUP
- ◯ MUSTARD
- ◯ MAYONAISE
- ◯ BBQ SAUCE

REVIEW

☆☆☆☆☆

NOTES

NAME OF HAMBURGER		MAKER

TOPPINGS
- ○ LETTUCE ○ ONION
- ○ BACON ○ PICKLES
- ○ TOMATO ○ CHEESE

TYPE OF BEEF

TYPE OF BUN

SEASONING

WEIGHT/CALORIES

COOKED

SIDES

COST

CONDIMENTS
- ○ KETCHUP
- ○ MUSTARD
- ○ MAYONAISE
- ○ BBQ SAUCE

REVIEW ☆ ☆ ☆ ☆ ☆

NOTES

NAME OF HAMBURGER

MAKER

TOPPINGS
- ○ LETTUCE ○ ONION
- ○ BACON ○ PICKLES
- ○ TOMATO ○ CHEESE

TYPE OF BEEF

TYPE OF BUN

SEASONING

WEIGHT/CALORIES

COOKED

SIDES

COST

CONDIMENTS
- ○ KETCHUP
- ○ MUSTARD
- ○ MAYONAISE
- ○ BBQ SAUCE

REVIEW   ☆☆☆☆☆

NOTES

NAME OF HAMBURGER

MAKER

TOGNINGS
- ( ) LETTUCE
- ( ) ONION
- ( ) BACON
- ( ) PICKLES
- ( ) TOMATO
- ( ) CHEESE

TYPE OF BEEF

TYPE OF BUN

SEASONING

WEIGHT/CALORIES

COOKED

SIDES

COST

CONDIMENTS
- ( ) KETCHUP
- ( ) MUSTARD
- ( ) MAYONAISE
- ( ) BBQ SAUCE

REVIEW

☆☆☆☆☆

NOTES

NAME OF HAMBURGER		MAKER

TOPPINGS
- ○ LETTUCE ○ ONION
- ○ BACON ○ PICKLES
- ○ TOMATO ○ CHEESE

TYPE OF BEEF

TYPE OF BUN

SEASONING

WEIGHT/CALORIES

COOKED

SIDES

COST

CONDIMENTS
- ○ KETCHUP
- ○ MUSTARD
- ○ MAYONAISE
- ○ BBQ SAUCE

REVIEW

☆☆☆☆☆

NOTES

NAME OF HAMBURGER

MAKER

TOPPINGS
- ( ) LETTUCE ( ) ONION
- ( ) BACON   ( ) PICKLES
- ( ) TOMATO   ( ) CHEESE

TYPE OF BEEF

TYPE OF BUN

SEASONING

WEIGHT/CALORIES

COOKED

SIDES

COST

CONDIMENTS
- ( ) KETCHUP
- ( ) MUSTARD
- ( ) MAYONAISE
- ( ) BBQ SAUCE

REVIEW

☆ ☆ ☆ ☆ ☆

NOTES

NAME OF HAMBURGER		MAKER

TOPPINGS
- ○ LETTUCE ○ ONION
- ○ BACON ○ PICKLES
- ○ TOMATO ○ CHEESE

TYPE OF BEEF	TYPE OF BUN
SEASONING	WEIGHT/CALORIES
COOKED	SIDES
COST	

CONDIMENTS
- ○ KETCHUP
- ○ MUSTARD
- ○ MAYONAISE
- ○ BBQ SAUCE

REVIEW ☆☆☆☆☆

NOTES

NAME OF HAMBURGER

MAKER

TOPPINGS
- ○ LETTUCE ○ ONION
- ○ BACON ○ PICKLES
- ○ TOMATO ○ CHEESE

TYPE OF BEEF

TYPE OF BUN

SEASONING

WEIGHT/CALORIES

COOKED

SIDES

COST

CONDIMENTS
- ○ KETCHUP
- ○ MUSTARD
- ○ MAYONAISE
- ○ BBQ SAUCE

REVIEW ☆☆☆☆☆

NOTES

NAME OF HAMBURGER

MAKER

TOPPINGS
- ( ) LETTUCE
- ( ) ONION
- ( ) BACON
- ( ) PICKLES
- ( ) TOMATO
- ( ) CHEESE

TYPE OF BEEF

TYPE OF BUN

SEASONING

WEIGHT/CALORIES

COOKED

SIDES

COST

CONDIMENTS
- ( ) KETCHUP
- ( ) MUSTARD
- ( ) MAYONAISE
- ( ) BBQ SAUCE

REVIEW

☆☆☆☆☆

NOTES

NAME OF HAMBURGER

MAKER

TOPPINGS
- ◯ LETTUCE ◯ ONION
- ◯ BACON ◯ PICKLES
- ◯ TOMATO ◯ CHEESE

TYPE OF BEEF

TYPE OF BUN

SEASONING

WEIGHT/CALORIES

COOKED

SIDES

COST

CONDIMENTS
- ◯ KETCHUP
- ◯ MUSTARD
- ◯ MAYONAISE
- ◯ BBQ SAUCE

REVIEW

☆☆☆☆☆

NOTES

NAME OF HAMBURGER

MAKER

TOPPINGS
- ( ) LETTUCE ( ) ONION
- ( ) BACON ( ) PICKLES
- ( ) TOMATO ( ) CHEESE

TYPE OF BEEF

TYPE OF BUN

SEASONING

WEIGHT/CALORIES

COOKED

SIDES

COST

CONDIMENTS
- ( ) KETCHUP
- ( ) MUSTARD
- ( ) MAYONAISE
- ( ) BBQ SAUCE

REVIEW

☆☆☆☆☆

NOTES

NAME OF HAMBURGER

MAKER

TOPPINGS
- ◯ LETTUCE ◯ ONION
- ◯ BACON ◯ PICKLES
- ◯ TOMATO ◯ CHEESE

TYPE OF BEEF

TYPE OF BUN

SEASONING

WEIGHT/CALORIES

COOKED

SIDES

COST

CONDIMENTS
- ◯ KETCHUP
- ◯ MUSTARD
- ◯ MAYONAISE
- ◯ BBQ SAUCE

REVIEW

☆☆☆☆☆

NOTES

Hamburger Review

NAME OF HAMBURGER

MAKER

TOPPINGS
- ◯ LETTUCE
- ◯ ONION
- ◯ BACON
- ◯ PICKLES
- ◯ TOMATO
- ◯ CHEESE

TYPE OF BEEF

TYPE OF BUN

SEASONING

WEIGHT/CALORIES

COOKED

SIDES

COST

CONDIMENTS
- ◯ KETCHUP
- ◯ MUSTARD
- ◯ MAYONAISE
- ◯ BBQ SAUCE

REVIEW

☆ ☆ ☆ ☆ ☆

NOTES

| NAME OF HAMBURGER | | MAKER |

TOPPINGS
- ( ) LETTUCE ( ) ONION
- ( ) BACON   ( ) PICKLES
- ( ) TOMATO   ( ) CHEESE

TYPE OF BEEF

TYPE OF BUN

SEASONING

WEIGHT/CALORIES

COOKED

SIDES

COST

CONDIMENTS
- ( ) KETCHUP
- ( ) MUSTARD
- ( ) MAYONAISE
- ( ) BBQ SAUCE

REVIEW   ☆☆☆☆☆

NOTES

Hamburger Review

NAME OF HAMBURGER

MAKER

TOPPINGS
- ( ) LETTUCE
- ( ) ONION
- ( ) BACON
- ( ) PICKLES
- ( ) TOMATO
- ( ) CHEESE

TYPE OF BEEF

TYPE OF BUN

SEASONING

WEIGHT/CALORIES

COOKED

SIDES

COST

CONDIMENTS
- ( ) KETCHUP
- ( ) MUSTARD
- ( ) MAYONAISE
- ( ) BBQ SAUCE

REVIEW

☆☆☆☆☆

NOTES

NAME OF HAMBURGER

MAKER

TOPPINGS
- ◯ LETTUCE ◯ ONION
- ◯ BACON ◯ PICKLES
- ◯ TOMATO ◯ CHEESE

TYPE OF BEEF

TYPE OF BUN

SEASONING

WEIGHT/CALORIES

COOKED

SIDES

COST

CONDIMENTS
- ◯ KETCHUP
- ◯ MUSTARD
- ◯ MAYONAISE
- ◯ BBQ SAUCE

REVIEW

☆☆☆☆☆

NOTES

Hamburger Review

NAME OF HAMBURGER

MAKER

TOPPINGS
- ◯ LETTUCE ◯ ONION
- ◯ BACON ◯ PICKLES
- ◯ TOMATO ◯ CHEESE

TYPE OF BEEF

TYPE OF BUN

SEASONING

WEIGHT/CALORIES

COOKED

SIDES

COST

CONDIMENTS
- ◯ KETCHUP
- ◯ MUSTARD
- ◯ MAYONAISE
- ◯ BBQ SAUCE

REVIEW

☆☆☆☆☆

NOTES

NAME OF HAMBURGER

MAKER

TOPPINGS
- ( ) LETTUCE ( ) ONION
- ( ) BACON ( ) PICKLES
- ( ) TOMATO ( ) CHEESE

TYPE OF BEEF

TYPE OF BUN

SEASONING

WEIGHT/CALORIES

COOKED

SIDES

COST

CONDIMENTS
- ( ) KETCHUP
- ( ) MUSTARD
- ( ) MAYONAISE
- ( ) BBQ SAUCE

REVIEW

☆☆☆☆☆

NOTES

NAME OF HAMBURGER		MAKER

TOPPINGS
- ( ) LETTUCE ( ) ONION
- ( ) BACON ( ) PICKLES
- ( ) TOMATO ( ) CHEESE

TYPE OF BEEF	TYPE OF BUN
SEASONING	WEIGHT/CALORIES
COOKED	SIDES
COST	

CONDIMENTS
- ( ) KETCHUP
- ( ) MUSTARD
- ( ) MAYONAISE
- ( ) BBQ SAUCE

REVIEW ☆☆☆☆☆

NOTES

NAME OF HAMBURGER		MAKER

TOPPINGS
- ( ) LETTUCE
- ( ) ONION
- ( ) BACON
- ( ) PICKLES
- ( ) TOMATO
- ( ) CHEESE

TYPE OF BEEF

TYPE OF BUN

SEASONING

WEIGHT/CALORIES

COOKED

SIDES

COST

CONDIMENTS
- ( ) KETCHUP
- ( ) MUSTARD
- ( ) MAYONAISE
- ( ) BBQ SAUCE

REVIEW   ☆ ☆ ☆ ☆ ☆

NOTES

NAME OF HAMBURGER

MAKER

TOPPINGS
- ( ) LETTUCE ( ) ONION
- ( ) BACON   ( ) PICKLES
- ( ) TOMATO   ( ) CHEESE

TYPE OF BEEF

TYPE OF BUN

SEASONING

WEIGHT/CALORIES

COOKED

SIDES

COST

CONDIMENTS
- ( ) KETCHUP
- ( ) MUSTARD
- ( ) MAYONAISE
- ( ) BBQ SAUCE

REVIEW

☆ ☆ ☆ ☆ ☆

NOTES

NAME OF HAMBURGER

MAKER

TOPPINGS
- ◯ LETTUCE ◯ ONION
- ◯ BACON ◯ PICKLES
- ◯ TOMATO ◯ CHEESE

TYPE OF BEEF

TYPE OF BUN

SEASONING

WEIGHT/CALORIES

COOKED

SIDES

COST

CONDIMENTS
- ◯ KETCHUP
- ◯ MUSTARD
- ◯ MAYONAISE
- ◯ BBQ SAUCE

REVIEW

☆☆☆☆☆

NOTES

NAME OF HAMBURGER

MAKER

TOPPINGS
- ( ) LETTUCE
- ( ) ONION
- ( ) BACON
- ( ) PICKLES
- ( ) TOMATO
- ( ) CHEESE

TYPE OF BEEF

TYPE OF BUN

SEASONING

WEIGHT/CALORIES

COOKED

SIDES

COST

CONDIMENTS
- ( ) KETCHUP
- ( ) MUSTARD
- ( ) MAYONAISE
- ( ) BBQ SAUCE

REVIEW

☆☆☆☆☆

NOTES

NAME OF HAMBURGER

MAKER

TOPPINGS

- ◯ LETTUCE
- ◯ ONION
- ◯ BACON
- ◯ PICKLES
- ◯ TOMATO
- ◯ CHEESE

TYPE OF BEEF

TYPE OF BUN

SEASONING

WEIGHT/CALORIES

COOKED

SIDES

COST

CONDIMENTS

- ◯ KETCHUP
- ◯ MUSTARD
- ◯ MAYONAISE
- ◯ BBQ SAUCE

REVIEW

☆☆☆☆☆

NOTES

NAME OF HAMBURGER		MAKER

TOPPINGS	TYPE OF BEEF	TYPE OF BUN
◯ LETTUCE ◯ ONION ◯ BACON ◯ PICKLES ◯ TOMATO ◯ CHEESE		
	SEASONING	WEIGHT/CALORIES
	COOKED	SIDES
	COST	

CONDIMENTS	REVIEW	☆☆☆☆☆
◯ KETCHUP ◯ MUSTARD ◯ MAYONAISE ◯ BBQ SAUCE		

NOTES

NAME OF HAMBURGER		MAKER

TOPPINGS
- ○ LETTUCE ○ ONION
- ○ BACON ○ PICKLES
- ○ TOMATO ○ CHEESE

TYPE OF BEEF

TYPE OF BUN

SEASONING

WEIGHT/CALORIES

COOKED

SIDES

COST

CONDIMENTS
- ○ KETCHUP
- ○ MUSTARD
- ○ MAYONAISE
- ○ BBQ SAUCE

REVIEW ☆☆☆☆☆

NOTES

NAME OF HAMBURGER

MAKER

TOPPINGS
- ⚪ LETTUCE
- ⚪ ONION
- ⚪ BACON
- ⚪ PICKLES
- ⚪ TOMATO
- ⚪ CHEESE

TYPE OF BEEF

TYPE OF BUN

SEASONING

WEIGHT/CALORIES

COOKED

SIDES

COST

CONDIMENTS
- ⚪ KETCHUP
- ⚪ MUSTARD
- ⚪ MAYONAISE
- ⚪ BBQ SAUCE

REVIEW

☆☆☆☆☆

NOTES

NAME OF HAMBURGER

MAKER

TOPPINGS
- ◯ LETTUCE ◯ ONION
- ◯ BACON ◯ PICKLES
- ◯ TOMATO ◯ CHEESE

TYPE OF BEEF

TYPE OF BUN

SEASONING

WEIGHT/CALORIES

COOKED

SIDES

COST

CONDIMENTS
- ◯ KETCHUP
- ◯ MUSTARD
- ◯ MAYONAISE
- ◯ BBQ SAUCE

REVIEW

☆☆☆☆☆

NOTES

NAME OF HAMBURGER		MAKER

TOPPINGS
- ○ LETTUCE ○ ONION
- ○ BACON ○ PICKLES
- ○ TOMATO ○ CHEESE

TYPE OF BEEF

TYPE OF BUN

SEASONING

WEIGHT/CALORIES

COOKED

SIDES

COST

CONDIMENTS
- ○ KETCHUP
- ○ MUSTARD
- ○ MAYONAISE
- ○ BBQ SAUCE

REVIEW ☆☆☆☆☆

NOTES

NAME OF HAMBURGER

MAKER

TOPPINGS

- ◯ LETTUCE
- ◯ ONION
- ◯ BACON
- ◯ PICKLES
- ◯ TOMATO
- ◯ CHEESE

TYPE OF BEEF

TYPE OF BUN

SEASONING

WEIGHT/CALORIES

COOKED

SIDES

COST

CONDIMENTS

- ◯ KETCHUP
- ◯ MUSTARD
- ◯ MAYONAISE
- ◯ BBQ SAUCE

REVIEW

☆☆☆☆☆

NOTES

Hamburger Review

NAME OF HAMBURGER

MAKER

TOPPINGS
- ◯ LETTUCE
- ◯ ONION
- ◯ BACON
- ◯ PICKLES
- ◯ TOMATO
- ◯ CHEESE

TYPE OF BEEF

TYPE OF BUN

SEASONING

WEIGHT/CALORIES

COOKED

SIDES

COST

CONDIMENTS
- ◯ KETCHUP
- ◯ MUSTARD
- ◯ MAYONAISE
- ◯ BBQ SAUCE

REVIEW

☆☆☆☆☆

NOTES

NAME OF HAMBURGER

MAKER

TOPPINGS
- ( ) LETTUCE ( ) ONION
- ( ) BACON ( ) PICKLES
- ( ) TOMATO ( ) CHEESE

TYPE OF BEEF

TYPE OF BUN

SEASONING

WEIGHT/CALORIES

COOKED

SIDES

COST

CONDIMENTS
- ( ) KETCHUP
- ( ) MUSTARD
- ( ) MAYONAISE
- ( ) BBQ SAUCE

REVIEW   ☆☆☆☆☆

NOTES

NAME OF HAMBURGER

MAKER

TOPPINGS
- ◯ LETTUCE ◯ ONION
- ◯ BACON ◯ PICKLES
- ◯ TOMATO ◯ CHEESE

TYPE OF BEEF

TYPE OF BUN

SEASONING

WEIGHT/CALORIES

COOKED

SIDES

COST

CONDIMENTS
- ◯ KETCHUP
- ◯ MUSTARD
- ◯ MAYONAISE
- ◯ BBQ SAUCE

REVIEW

☆☆☆☆☆

NOTES

NAME OF HAMBURGER

MAKER

TOPPINGS
- ◯ LETTUCE ◯ ONION
- ◯ BACON ◯ PICKLES
- ◯ TOMATO ◯ CHEESE

TYPE OF BEEF

TYPE OF BUN

SEASONING

WEIGHT/CALORIES

COOKED

SIDES

COST

CONDIMENTS
- ◯ KETCHUP
- ◯ MUSTARD
- ◯ MAYONAISE
- ◯ BBQ SAUCE

REVIEW

☆☆☆☆☆

NOTES

Hamburger Review

NAME OF HAMBURGER

MAKER

TOPPINGS
- ○ LETTUCE
- ○ ONION
- ○ BACON
- ○ PICKLES
- ○ TOMATO
- ○ CHEESE

TYPE OF BEEF

TYPE OF BUN

SEASONING

WEIGHT/CALORIES

COOKED

SIDES

COST

CONDIMENTS
- ○ KETCHUP
- ○ MUSTARD
- ○ MAYONAISE
- ○ BBQ SAUCE

REVIEW

☆☆☆☆☆

NOTES

NAME OF HAMBURGER

MAKER

TOPPINGS
- ◯ LETTUCE ◯ ONION
- ◯ BACON ◯ PICKLES
- ◯ TOMATO ◯ CHEESE

TYPE OF BEEF

TYPE OF BUN

SEASONING

WEIGHT/CALORIES

COOKED

SIDES

COST

CONDIMENTS
- ◯ KETCHUP
- ◯ MUSTARD
- ◯ MAYONAISE
- ◯ BBQ SAUCE

REVIEW

☆☆☆☆☆

NOTES

Hamburger Review

NAME OF HAMBURGER

MAKER

TOPPINGS
- ◯ LETTUCE ◯ ONION
- ◯ BACON ◯ PICKLES
- ◯ TOMATO ◯ CHEESE

TYPE OF BEEF

TYPE OF BUN

SEASONING

WEIGHT/CALORIES

COOKED

SIDES

COST

CONDIMENTS
- ◯ KETCHUP
- ◯ MUSTARD
- ◯ MAYONAISE
- ◯ BBQ SAUCE

REVIEW

☆☆☆☆☆

NOTES

NAME OF HAMBURGER

MAKER

TOPPINGS
- ◯ LETTUCE ◯ ONION
- ◯ BACON ◯ PICKLES
- ◯ TOMATO ◯ CHEESE

TYPE OF BEEF

TYPE OF BUN

SEASONING

WEIGHT/CALORIES

COOKED

SIDES

COST

CONDIMENTS
- ◯ KETCHUP
- ◯ MUSTARD
- ◯ MAYONAISE
- ◯ BBQ SAUCE

REVIEW

☆☆☆☆☆

NOTES

NAME OF HAMBURGER

MAKER

TOPPINGS
- ( ) LETTUCE ( ) ONION
- ( ) BACON ( ) PICKLES
- ( ) TOMATO ( ) CHEESE

TYPE OF BEEF

TYPE OF BUN

SEASONING

WEIGHT/CALORIES

COOKED

SIDES

COST

CONDIMENTS
- ( ) KETCHUP
- ( ) MUSTARD
- ( ) MAYONAISE
- ( ) BBQ SAUCE

REVIEW

☆☆☆☆☆

NOTES

NAME OF HAMBURGER

MAKER

TOPPINGS
- ◯ LETTUCE ◯ ONION
- ◯ BACON ◯ PICKLES
- ◯ TOMATO ◯ CHEESE

TYPE OF BEEF

TYPE OF BUN

SEASONING

WEIGHT/CALORIES

COOKED

SIDES

COST

CONDIMENTS
- ◯ KETCHUP
- ◯ MUSTARD
- ◯ MAYONAISE
- ◯ BBQ SAUCE

REVIEW

☆☆☆☆☆

NOTES

Hamburger Log

NAME OF HAMBURGER

MAKER

TOPPINGS
- ◯ LETTUCE
- ◯ ONION
- ◯ BACON
- ◯ PICKLES
- ◯ TOMATO
- ◯ CHEESE

TYPE OF BEEF

TYPE OF BUN

SEASONING

WEIGHT/CALORIES

COOKED

SIDES

COST

CONDIMENTS
- ◯ KETCHUP
- ◯ MUSTARD
- ◯ MAYONAISE
- ◯ BBQ SAUCE

REVIEW

☆☆☆☆☆

NOTES

| NAME OF HAMBURGER | | MAKER |

TOPPINGS
- ◯ LETTUCE ◯ ONION
- ◯ BACON ◯ PICKLES
- ◯ TOMATO ◯ CHEESE

TYPE OF BEEF

TYPE OF BUN

SEASONING

WEIGHT/CALORIES

COOKED

SIDES

COST

CONDIMENTS
- ◯ KETCHUP
- ◯ MUSTARD
- ◯ MAYONAISE
- ◯ BBQ SAUCE

REVIEW

☆☆☆☆☆

NOTES

NAME OF HAMBURGER

MAKER

TOPPINGS
- ◯ LETTUCE ◯ ONION
- ◯ BACON ◯ PICKLES
- ◯ TOMATO ◯ CHEESE

TYPE OF BEEF

TYPE OF BUN

SEASONING

WEIGHT/CALORIES

COOKED

SIDES

COST

CONDIMENTS
- ◯ KETCHUP
- ◯ MUSTARD
- ◯ MAYONAISE
- ◯ BBQ SAUCE

REVIEW

☆☆☆☆☆

NOTES

NAME OF HAMBURGER

MAKER

TOPPINGS
- ◯ LETTUCE
- ◯ ONION
- ◯ BACON
- ◯ PICKLES
- ◯ TOMATO
- ◯ CHEESE

TYPE OF BEEF

TYPE OF BUN

SEASONING

WEIGHT/CALORIES

COOKED

SIDES

COST

CONDIMENTS
- ◯ KETCHUP
- ◯ MUSTARD
- ◯ MAYONAISE
- ◯ BBQ SAUCE

REVIEW

☆☆☆☆☆

NOTES

NAME OF HAMBURGER		MAKER

TOPPINGS
- ○ LETTUCE ○ ONION
- ○ BACON ○ PICKLES
- ○ TOMATO ○ CHEESE

TYPE OF BEEF	TYPE OF BUN
SEASONING	WEIGHT/CALORIES
COOKED	SIDES
COST	

CONDIMENTS
- ○ KETCHUP
- ○ MUSTARD
- ○ MAYONAISE
- ○ BBQ SAUCE

REVIEW ☆☆☆☆☆

NOTES

NAME OF HAMBURGER

MAKER

TOPPINGS
- ◯ LETTUCE ◯ ONION
- ◯ BACON ◯ PICKLES
- ◯ TOMATO ◯ CHEESE

TYPE OF BEEF

TYPE OF BUN

SEASONING

WEIGHT/CALORIES

COOKED

SIDES

COST

CONDIMENTS
- ◯ KETCHUP
- ◯ MUSTARD
- ◯ MAYONAISE
- ◯ BBQ SAUCE

REVIEW

☆☆☆☆☆

NOTES

NAME OF HAMBURGER		MAKER

TOPPINGS
- ○ LETTUCE ○ ONION
- ○ BACON ○ PICKLES
- ○ TOMATO ○ CHEESE

TYPE OF BEEF	TYPE OF BUN
SEASONING	WEIGHT/CALORIES
COOKED	SIDES
COST	

CONDIMENTS
- ○ KETCHUP
- ○ MUSTARD
- ○ MAYONAISE
- ○ BBQ SAUCE

REVIEW ☆☆☆☆☆

NOTES

NAME OF HAMBURGER

MAKER

TOPPINGS
- ◯ LETTUCE
- ◯ ONION
- ◯ BACON
- ◯ PICKLES
- ◯ TOMATO
- ◯ CHEESE

TYPE OF BEEF

TYPE OF BUN

SEASONING

WEIGHT/CALORIES

COOKED

SIDES

COST

CONDIMENTS
- ◯ KETCHUP
- ◯ MUSTARD
- ◯ MAYONAISE
- ◯ BBQ SAUCE

REVIEW

☆☆☆☆☆

NOTES

Hamburger Review

NAME OF HAMBURGER		MAKER

TOPPINGS
- ○ LETTUCE
- ○ ONION
- ○ BACON
- ○ PICKLES
- ○ TOMATO
- ○ CHEESE

TYPE OF BEEF	TYPE OF BUN
SEASONING	WEIGHT/CALORIES
COOKED	SIDES
COST	

CONDIMENTS
- ○ KETCHUP
- ○ MUSTARD
- ○ MAYONAISE
- ○ BBQ SAUCE

REVIEW ☆☆☆☆☆

NOTES

| NAME OF HAMBURGER | | MAKER |

TOPPINGS
- ◯ LETTUCE ◯ ONION
- ◯ BACON ◯ PICKLES
- ◯ TOMATO ◯ CHEESE

TYPE OF BEEF

TYPE OF BUN

SEASONING

WEIGHT/CALORIES

COOKED

SIDES

COST

CONDIMENTS
- ◯ KETCHUP
- ◯ MUSTARD
- ◯ MAYONAISE
- ◯ BBQ SAUCE

REVIEW ☆☆☆☆☆

NOTES

NAME OF HAMBURGER

MAKER

TOPPINGS
- ◯ LETTUCE
- ◯ ONION
- ◯ BACON
- ◯ PICKLES
- ◯ TOMATO
- ◯ CHEESE

TYPE OF BEEF

TYPE OF BUN

SEASONING

WEIGHT/CALORIES

COOKED

SIDES

COST

CONDIMENTS
- ◯ KETCHUP
- ◯ MUSTARD
- ◯ MAYONAISE
- ◯ BBQ SAUCE

REVIEW

☆☆☆☆☆

NOTES

NAME OF HAMBURGER

MAKER

TOPPINGS
- ◯ LETTUCE ◯ ONION
- ◯ BACON ◯ PICKLES
- ◯ TOMATO ◯ CHEESE

TYPE OF BEEF

TYPE OF BUN

SEASONING

WEIGHT/CALORIES

COOKED

SIDES

COST

CONDIMENTS
- ◯ KETCHUP
- ◯ MUSTARD
- ◯ MAYONAISE
- ◯ BBQ SAUCE

REVIEW

☆☆☆☆☆

NOTES

Hamburger Review

NAME OF HAMBURGER

MAKER

TOPPINGS
- ◯ LETTUCE ◯ ONION
- ◯ BACON ◯ PICKLES
- ◯ TOMATO ◯ CHEESE

TYPE OF BEEF

TYPE OF BUN

SEASONING

WEIGHT/CALORIES

COOKED

SIDES

COST

CONDIMENTS
- ◯ KETCHUP
- ◯ MUSTARD
- ◯ MAYONAISE
- ◯ BBQ SAUCE

REVIEW   ☆☆☆☆☆

NOTES

| NAME OF HAMBURGER | MAKER |

TOPPINGS
- ○ LETTUCE ○ ONION
- ○ BACON   ○ PICKLES
- ○ TOMATO   ○ CHEESE

TYPE OF BEEF

TYPE OF BUN

SEASONING

WEIGHT/CALORIES

COOKED

SIDES

COST

CONDIMENTS
- ○ KETCHUP
- ○ MUSTARD
- ○ MAYONAISE
- ○ BBQ SAUCE

REVIEW ☆☆☆☆☆

NOTES

NAME OF HAMBURGER		**MAKER**

TOPPINGS
- ( ) LETTUCE ( ) ONION
- ( ) BACON ( ) PICKLES
- ( ) TOMATO ( ) CHEESE

TYPE OF BEEF

TYPE OF BUN

SEASONING

WEIGHT/CALORIES

COOKED

SIDES

COST

CONDIMENTS
- ( ) KETCHUP
- ( ) MUSTARD
- ( ) MAYONAISE
- ( ) BBQ SAUCE

REVIEW

☆☆☆☆☆

NOTES

NAME OF HAMBURGER

MAKER

TOPPINGS
- ( ) LETTUCE ( ) ONION
- ( ) BACON   ( ) PICKLES
- ( ) TOMATO   ( ) CHEESE

TYPE OF BEEF

TYPE OF BUN

SEASONING

WEIGHT/CALORIES

COOKED

SIDES

COST

CONDIMENTS
- ( ) KETCHUP
- ( ) MUSTARD
- ( ) MAYONAISE
- ( ) BBQ SAUCE

REVIEW

☆ ☆ ☆ ☆ ☆

NOTES

NAME OF HAMBURGER

MAKER

TOPPINGS
- ( ) LETTUCE
- ( ) ONION
- ( ) BACON
- ( ) PICKLES
- ( ) TOMATO
- ( ) CHEESE

TYPE OF BEEF

TYPE OF BUN

SEASONING

WEIGHT/CALORIES

COOKED

SIDES

COST

CONDIMENTS
- ( ) KETCHUP
- ( ) MUSTARD
- ( ) MAYONAISE
- ( ) BBQ SAUCE

REVIEW ☆☆☆☆☆

NOTES

NAME OF HAMBURGER

MAKER

TOPPINGS
- ☐ LETTUCE
- ☐ ONION
- ☐ BACON
- ☐ PICKLES
- ☐ TOMATO
- ☐ CHEESE

TYPE OF BEEF

TYPE OF BUN

SEASONING

WEIGHT/CALORIES

COOKED

SIDES

COST

CONDIMENTS
- ☐ KETCHUP
- ☐ MUSTARD
- ☐ MAYONAISE
- ☐ BBQ SAUCE

REVIEW   ☆☆☆☆☆

NOTES

NAME OF HAMBURGER		MAKER
TOPPINGS ◯ LETTUCE ◯ ONION ◯ BACON ◯ PICKLES ◯ TOMATO ◯ CHEESE	TYPE OF BEEF	TYPE OF BUN
	SEASONING	WEIGHT/CALORIES
	COOKED	SIDES
	COST	
CONDIMENTS ◯ KETCHUP ◯ MUSTARD ◯ MAYONAISE ◯ BBQ SAUCE	REVIEW	☆☆☆☆☆

NOTES

NAME OF HAMBURGER		MAKER

TOPPINGS
- ○ LETTUCE
- ○ ONION
- ○ BACON
- ○ PICKLES
- ○ TOMATO
- ○ CHEESE

TYPE OF BEEF

TYPE OF BUN

SEASONING

WEIGHT/CALORIES

COOKED

SIDES

COST

CONDIMENTS
- ○ KETCHUP
- ○ MUSTARD
- ○ MAYONAISE
- ○ BBQ SAUCE

REVIEW ☆☆☆☆☆

NOTES

NAME OF HAMBURGER		MAKER

TOPPINGS
- ○ LETTUCE ○ ONION
- ○ BACON ○ PICKLES
- ○ TOMATO ○ CHEESE

TYPE OF BEEF	TYPE OF BUN
SEASONING	WEIGHT/CALORIES
COOKED	SIDES
COST	

CONDIMENTS
- ○ KETCHUP
- ○ MUSTARD
- ○ MAYONAISE
- ○ BBQ SAUCE

REVIEW ☆☆☆☆☆

NOTES

NAME OF HAMBURGER

MAKER

TOPPINGS
- ( ) LETTUCE ( ) ONION
- ( ) BACON ( ) PICKLES
- ( ) TOMATO ( ) CHEESE

TYPE OF BEEF

TYPE OF BUN

SEASONING

WEIGHT/CALORIES

COOKED

SIDES

COST

CONDIMENTS
- ( ) KETCHUP
- ( ) MUSTARD
- ( ) MAYONAISE
- ( ) BBQ SAUCE

REVIEW

☆☆☆☆☆

NOTES

NAME OF HAMBURGER

MAKER

TOPPINGS
- ◯ LETTUCE ◯ ONION
- ◯ BACON ◯ PICKLES
- ◯ TOMATO ◯ CHEESE

TYPE OF BEEF

TYPE OF BUN

SEASONING

WEIGHT/CALORIES

COOKED

SIDES

COST

CONDIMENTS
- ◯ KETCHUP
- ◯ MUSTARD
- ◯ MAYONAISE
- ◯ BBQ SAUCE

REVIEW ☆☆☆☆☆

NOTES

NAME OF HAMBURGER

MAKER

TOPPINGS
- ◯ LETTUCE ◯ ONION
- ◯ BACON ◯ PICKLES
- ◯ TOMATO ◯ CHEESE

TYPE OF BEEF

TYPE OF BUN

SEASONING

WEIGHT/CALORIES

COOKED

SIDES

COST

CONDIMENTS
- ◯ KETCHUP
- ◯ MUSTARD
- ◯ MAYONAISE
- ◯ BBQ SAUCE

REVIEW

☆☆☆☆☆

NOTES

NAME OF HAMBURGER

MAKER

TOPPINGS
- ○ LETTUCE ○ ONION
- ○ BACON ○ PICKLES
- ○ TOMATO ○ CHEESE

TYPE OF BEEF

TYPE OF BUN

SEASONING

WEIGHT/CALORIES

COOKED

SIDES

COST

CONDIMENTS
- ○ KETCHUP
- ○ MUSTARD
- ○ MAYONAISE
- ○ BBQ SAUCE

REVIEW

☆☆☆☆☆

NOTES

NAME OF HAMBURGER

MAKER

TOPPINGS
- ◯ LETTUCE ◯ ONION
- ◯ BACON ◯ PICKLES
- ◯ TOMATO ◯ CHEESE

TYPE OF BEEF

TYPE OF BUN

SEASONING

WEIGHT/CALORIES

COOKED

SIDES

COST

CONDIMENTS
- ◯ KETCHUP
- ◯ MUSTARD
- ◯ MAYONAISE
- ◯ BBQ SAUCE

REVIEW

☆☆☆☆☆

NOTES

NAME OF HAMBURGER		MAKER
TOPPINGS ○ LETTUCE ○ ONION ○ BACON ○ PICKLES ○ TOMATO ○ CHEESE	**TYPE OF BEEF**	**TYPE OF BUN**
	SEASONING	**WEIGHT/CALORIES**
	COOKED	**SIDES**
	COST	
CONDIMENTS ○ KETCHUP ○ MUSTARD ○ MAYONAISE ○ BBQ SAUCE	**REVIEW**	☆☆☆☆☆

NOTES

NAME OF HAMBURGER

MAKER

TOPPINGS
- ◯ LETTUCE ◯ ONION
- ◯ BACON ◯ PICKLES
- ◯ TOMATO ◯ CHEESE

TYPE OF BEEF

TYPE OF BUN

SEASONING

WEIGHT/CALORIES

COOKED

SIDES

COST

CONDIMENTS
- ◯ KETCHUP
- ◯ MUSTARD
- ◯ MAYONAISE
- ◯ BBQ SAUCE

REVIEW

☆☆☆☆☆

NOTES

NAME OF HAMBURGER

MAKER

TOPPINGS
- ◯ LETTUCE
- ◯ ONION
- ◯ BACON
- ◯ PICKLES
- ◯ TOMATO
- ◯ CHEESE

TYPE OF BEEF

TYPE OF BUN

SEASONING

WEIGHT/CALORIES

COOKED

SIDES

COST

CONDIMENTS
- ◯ KETCHUP
- ◯ MUSTARD
- ◯ MAYONAISE
- ◯ BBQ SAUCE

REVIEW

☆☆☆☆☆

NOTES

NAME OF HAMBURGER

MAKER

TOPPINGS
- ○ LETTUCE
- ○ ONION
- ○ BACON
- ○ PICKLES
- ○ TOMATO
- ○ CHEESE

TYPE OF BEEF

TYPE OF BUN

SEASONING

WEIGHT/CALORIES

COOKED

SIDES

COST

CONDIMENTS
- ○ KETCHUP
- ○ MUSTARD
- ○ MAYONAISE
- ○ BBQ SAUCE

REVIEW

☆☆☆☆☆

NOTES

Hamburger Review

NAME OF HAMBURGER

MAKER

TOPPINGS
- ( ) LETTUCE ( ) ONION
- ( ) BACON ( ) PICKLES
- ( ) TOMATO ( ) CHEESE

TYPE OF BEEF

TYPE OF BUN

SEASONING

WEIGHT/CALORIES

COOKED

SIDES

COST

CONDIMENTS
- ( ) KETCHUP
- ( ) MUSTARD
- ( ) MAYONAISE
- ( ) BBQ SAUCE

REVIEW ☆☆☆☆☆

NOTES

NAME OF HAMBURGER

MAKER

TOPPINGS
- ( ) LETTUCE
- ( ) ONION
- ( ) BACON
- ( ) PICKLES
- ( ) TOMATO
- ( ) CHEESE

TYPE OF BEEF

TYPE OF BUN

SEASONING

WEIGHT/CALORIES

COOKED

SIDES

COST

CONDIMENTS
- ( ) KETCHUP
- ( ) MUSTARD
- ( ) MAYONAISE
- ( ) BBQ SAUCE

REVIEW ☆☆☆☆☆

NOTES

NAME OF HAMBURGER

MAKER

TOPPINGS
- ○ LETTUCE ○ ONION
- ○ BACON ○ PICKLES
- ○ TOMATO ○ CHEESE

TYPE OF BEEF

TYPE OF BUN

SEASONING

WEIGHT/CALORIES

COOKED

SIDES

COST

CONDIMENTS
- ○ KETCHUP
- ○ MUSTARD
- ○ MAYONAISE
- ○ BBQ SAUCE

REVIEW

☆☆☆☆☆

NOTES

Made in the USA
Monee, IL
17 December 2021